# A Result of Socialism

# A Result of Socialism

*How Seventy Years Of Socialism Has Ruined Ukraine*

Hans K. Paladini

**To order additional copies of this book, contact:**
Xlibris Corporation
1-888-795-4274
www.Xlibris.com
Orders@Xlibris.com
103538

# CONTENTS

# FOREWORD

As the fires burn in London we see another result of socialism unfold before our very eyes. It is not past history but a current event. They are a disgruntled class of people that have been raised up as wards of the state. These hooligans have now broken loose like angry children when something has been taken away from them. England as well as the rest of Western Europe has had this cradle to grave social system the reallocates wealth from the working people to a group of people who have no motivation to work ever!

After decades of living under that system, of course they will riot when the government must take it away from them or go broke. It will happen here if the march towards socialism isn't turned around. When a group eat, drink and have sex and the government subsidizes it by taxing the working people then of course you will have this reaction because these people are no different than animals in the zoo.

This book is dedicated to

the memory of

**Viktor Sherbakov**

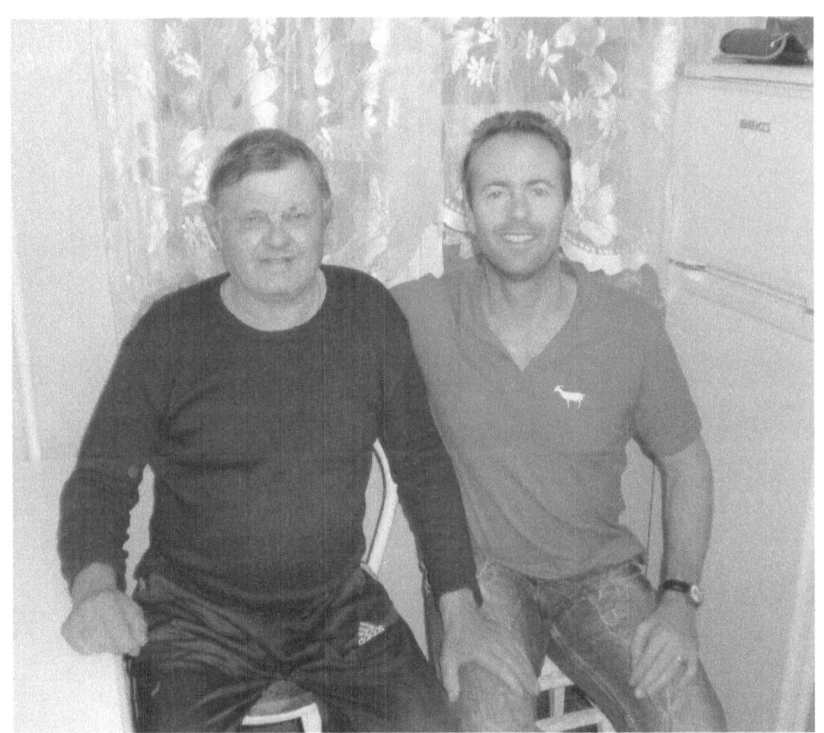

# LIFE ON THE MARSHRUTE

If you are brave enough to choose to go the Ukraine there are number of things one needs to know. The Ukraine is a long way from the United States in both distance and culture. The best description of the feeling for someone who has never been to the Ukraine before is it is the former Soviet Union. The look and feel of the country is that it has been dragged down by seventy years of atheistic communism. Besides the outward appearance of aging infrastructure and suffering economy, the people are in many ways left without hope.

A marchrute taxi.

Life in the Ukraine is hard. People must live day to day often wonder where their next meal will come from. We have it much better in the U.S, and for me personally it was a shock to see such poverty. I have travelled to many places but for me the Ukraine was one of the places that were sad to see in such bad shape.

If you don't speak Russian or Ukrainian it is best to take a translator with you because most people don't speak English and when they do, they will often times try to take advantage of you. If you are from the west they will often look at you like a walking ATM. It is best to take a native speaker with you whenever you are in the Ukraine. It can save you a lot of problems like being robbed by the police! But we won't get into that.

A old Marchrute still in operation

The mode of transportation in the Ukraine is the Marshrute Taxi or Marshrutka. This is a small bus that fits between ten to twenty people and covers both metropolitan and rural routes. The cost is minimal usually two Ukrainian Hrivnas (approx. twenty cents) so everyone can ride it especially in and around the city. You usually pay when you get off but there are cities like Nikolaev that you must pay when you get in. If there are twenty seats don't be surprised the forty people will be in the bus. Just because the door opens and it looks full doesn't mean more people won't get in. The personal space on the Marshrute Taxi is just inches. You will find out real quick who didn't shower that day.

But having said this, I found riding these Marshrutes liberating and enjoyable, at least when it was not hot. One could get on at any station and get around throughout the city with ease. For someone from Northern California who got used to the car culture this form of public transportation was just different to say the least.

The Marshrute Taxi like any form of public transportation is a microcosm of society. Just like the subway is in any major American city, the Marshrute is a representation of the society of the Ukraine. One will see the elderly going to market, the youth going to school, and many going to work.

What I remember most about the Marshrute is the times that a dog got sick behind us or the time I had to smell and see a village ladie's hairy armpits for ten kilometers on a hot day. These seem to be the things that stay in your mind.

The way my wife and I experienced Ukraine was on a tight budget and I don't regret it at all. I believe if one travels through countries staying in first class hotels and eating in fine restaurants and being chauffeured around, takes the real feel of the country away from the traveler.

# FIRST IMPRESSIONS

An old Lada at the settlement

When I mentioned in the first section that the Ukraine looks like a post Soviet Union country, what I meant was the country actually looks like how the Soviet Union actually was. Many things just haven't changed and improved. Little has changed structurally and at first impression it looks like a great place to film a movie about the Soviet Union. Most buildings are sterile white cement structures made to look like one another. They are the same in any city you go. I had seen this once before in the late nineties when I was in the former East Germany. They are the pride and joy of socialist style architecture. But after the Iron Curtain came down the Germans quickly tore them down and modernized in most places. The reason they build this way was because they didn't want any city to look better than any other city. They couldn't afford people becoming disgruntled because back then people were told where to live and where to work so if they visited their relatives or friends in another city they would want to move to a better place. This is a typical human response to improving one's life. But in Soviet style communism the work force needed be sent to where they could be used and freedom to pursue a better wage was practically nonexistent. What they told people back then were wherever you go in the great Soviet Union you will feel at home since it looked the same. They even named many street names the same. This kept people somewhat content since many were assigned a place to live and a work place and were not free to turn it down. This is socialism at it greatest extent of power, controlling people's lives and their vary actions.

The streets are full of old buses and Marshrute Taxis many of them twenty plus years or older. You can see cars like Ladas, Skodas, and Zaporozhets which were common cars in the Soviet Union. It is interesting if you are in to old eastern European cars. They are little boxes made with a lot more steel than most American cars and the Ukrainian mechanics must be magicians to keep these cars running for twenty to thirty years. Some are so old I was told that there are no more spare parts but they make their own spare parts. They somehow keep these cars running. We rode in many that were used as taxis.

The taxi drivers are a mixed bag. Some are not so friendly and downright angry and some are friendly and funny. Often their English is limited but since my wife is fluent in Russian and Ukrainian we didn't have a problem asking questions when visiting a new city. Like in most cities worldwide taxi drivers are the ones who know everything about their cities from restaurants to sights.

One can see many old cars still in operation

# INFRASTRUCTURE

The main reason I am writing this book to an American audience is not just to give them a little taste of what a former Soviet Bloc country is like, since many Americans never travel outside the States. But also to give them a warning what seventy years of socialistic atheism can do to a country economically, socially and spiritually.

A typical Soviet style building

Many economic policies that have been instituted by the Obama administration recently here in the U.S. have alarmed and upset many people. The Keynesian idea of big government reallocating wealth is very similar to the philosophy that Lenin had about redistribution of his country's wealth and resources.

Old floodlights in Kherson stadium

A radio signal blocking tower from the time
of the Soviet Union in Lvov

The first thing one notices about Ukraine when one lands in Kiev or Odessa is they are small old airports built during the era when very few were allowed to leave the country for any reason. They are built with the typical cement block style and not modern terminals. The runways are small and are often snowed under during storms which I experienced when flying into Kiev. I waited an hour and a half for my bags to be unloaded from the plane and getting out of the airport was a mess. The idea of customer service is gone as soon as your feet hit the ground. Not just the infrastructure is from the Soviet Union but the mentality is from the Soviet Union. For example, our Lufthansa plane got us there to Kiev in a snow storm that was no worse than the one we left in Munich. We landed on time and the pilot was able to ease the machine onto the tarmac surprisingly easy. But we had to wait thirty minutes before they could get a bus to us to shuttle us to the terminal. The Lufthansa crew apologized to us for the delay but they were not at fault. Finally the shuttle arrived and we loaded onto it for the ride to the terminal. With the experience at customs which was pure bedlam, I mean no one knew how to form lines. Then finally the long wait for the baggage that I mentioned before. I believe the reason why the airports were in such bad shape is that anything a government runs when it comes to business does not work in the long run. When the workers are working for the government they are low paid and have little motivation and do as little as possible. There is no motivation to improve, and it is very difficult to be fired. The idea that there are just two "international" airports in the Ukraine, Kiev Borispol and Odessa, make for little competition and little need to improve services for air travelers. There are other airports in Ukraine but one must travel through these two to get to the other ones when coming from Western Europe. It is strange for a country larger than the size of Texas to have only two fully functioning airports. The Ukraine is 233,090 square miles.

I already mentioned the famous Marshrute buses and taxis in the first two chapters. The variety of roads they have to travel on are anything from freeways, more like highways than modern type autobahns like in Germany, to dirt roads. When one travels by Marshrute or car in the Ukraine one will travel all types of roads many of which haven't been repaired in decades.

Another mode of travel and a preferred one by this author for long distances in the Ukraine is by rail. I am a fan of train travel and have done it many times through Europe and the U.S. But even the most hardcore train buff will find it a bit tedious travelling through Ukraine by train. The cars and engines are for the most part from the time of the Soviet Union and so are the stations. It was like going back in time some thirty years.

There are three classes for Ukrainian rail which is the government owned rail company. V.I.P is the nicest class and one gets two beds in a private room which is comfortable for a long overnight journey. It ran from $50-$100 for an overnight trip depending on the distance. The next class down is called coupé. This is a similar room as VIP class but there are four beds so you often have to share with a stranger which at times is O.K. and at other times is a bit too close. We found that if we bought all four beds and folded up the top ones it was comfortable, private and less expensive than VIP class. The last class is "platzkarte", this class is basically just wooden benches and an open sleeping area with no privacy. I wouldn't recommend this class to foreigners. It is hot, smelly and filled with disgruntled people too.

Since the trains are so old it makes a trip across Ukraine, which as I mentioned before is a very large country. 233.090 square miles very long. Most trips are overnight depending on distance. The 200kph train trips of Western Europe are replaced by the slow moving Ukrainian train that probably reaches top speeds of 80 kph.

I asked one conductor how old is this train that we were riding on as I looked down at the whole in the floor watching the tracks go by. She said, "Older than me." She looked about thirty to forty years old. My suspicions were answered. Not that a train forty years old couldn't work, but the repairs needed to be done on it. This one was in need of some repairs. I must say the service on the trains was still good and for the most part the train workers were hard working and efficient. I guess there is something to be said about working on the railroad, always on the go, seeing one's country and never staying at one station very long.

Lenin can be found in most post Soviet cities. Here he stands
in the largest square in Europe which is in Kharkov

As far as the station workers go it was a different story. They work in small windows for long hours probably not getting paid very much. Many of them were ornery and miserable. They won't answer any questions and if they did they did angrily. My wife and I once asked a question about train times and got yelled at from the lady in the window. They don't know how to process a credit card transaction even though they are set up for it so we had to pay cash even though we would of liked to pay with a credit card. Credit cards are still a bit foreign in the Ukraine. Also a warning about the ticket lines at train stations. There is no such thing. If you start at the back of a line you will stay at the back. Start farther up and cut whenever you can, because you will be cut in front of anyway. Hold on to your wallet and don't be too polite. This will tell everyone that you are a foreigner and you will have problems. The Ukrainians don't form lines very well and like to slip in front whenever they can. Train stations weren't my favorite place in Ukraine but once I was on the train it was O.K.

One of the more interesting happenings that occurred at a train station in Kherson was when we were boarding a train to Kiev around midnight and there was a usually large police presence at the station. They had about ten officers with guns and a couple of dogs. When we tried to get in our wagon we were halted while they were trying to load a large box about the size of a T.V. on the train. What I noticed was that three grown men had a hard time loading it on board. Then we noticed that an uninformed swarthy man came up to the officer in charge and said," his boss had talked to the officer's boss and wanted them not to ship the box to Kiev." The officer replied," He hadn't received the message and they would continue to ship the package." Just at that time as a fourth officer help load the box onto the train I heard the contents of the box clank like something metallic was in there. The stranger in black leather, disgruntled, disappeared into the cold night and I thought to myself what could be so heavy? Lead or gold is that heavy. I wondered as they finally got the box loaded and put into the first cabin. Three officers accompanied the box that night to Kiev. Who knows what was in there but obviously something very valuable?

# THE ECONOMY

One of the things that were evident in the Ukraine to someone that has an economics degree was the high rate of unemployment and little or no unemployment insurance. It wasn't like many western European countries that had a high number of people on unemployment because they make enough to live on so there is no motivation for them to get off. To Americans this sounds familiar when the Obama administration extended the unemployment benefits to ninety nine weeks! No, in the Ukraine it isn't like that. There are no unemployment benefits or safety nets in place. Yet people still didn't have work. Many people would try to start their own businesses or set up stands at the local bazaar and sell whatever they could. I liked the bazaars for the most part, even though they were crowded and loud, and one would have to watch his step in the crowded alleys. It was for me pure capitalism, or capitalism gone wild!

The people would sell everything from vegetables to shoes in either container type stores or just from a table. Each town or city had one or more. Some were large and others not. You could find just about everything and for a fair price. It was also cash only so one should leave his Visa at home. The people were trying to make it on their own and I liked the spirit. Since the former Soviet Union employed many people in government run factories and farms and many now are shut down the people have seemed to have taken it into their own hands and created a retail service sector of their own. Some of the goods are local and others from faraway places like China since it is cheaper to import than produce locally. This situation is similar to that in the U.S. about importing rather than producing it ourselves.

As for taxes there is a twenty percent sales tax that the government uses as a pension fund for the retirement age people. But after looking around I wonder where all the money goes that the government brings in.

Another theme that keeps reoccurring when one is in the Ukraine is the idea of customer service or lack of it. In many places you won't find good customer service of course there is always the exception. In many government owned stores and large chains you will get the rudimentary service but nothing like in the states. I attribute this to lack of training and seventy years of socialist mentality that would provide one bakery, for example, and no competition. So one would have to go there if you wanted bread and there was no reason to be nice to you. You were just a number in the line. This mentality is slowly disappearing through training and the better understanding of capitalistic ideas that if you don't take care of your customers then someone else will and you will go out of business.

The use of credit cards is new there and more and more places are taking them but cash is still king. It is not uncommon to find older workers who are unfamiliar with how to complete a credit card transaction and often young people too. In the Ukraine they still take the credit card from you and swipe it themselves and then have to put in a code. Then the transaction goes through but often takes longer than cash transactions. Much like it was in the U.S. twenty years ago. We often had cashiers tell us that the system won't complete the transaction, do you have cash? We were also told that the system is down for a couple of days at some stores.

Theses inefficiencies can hurt sales, especially from foreigners who often use credit cards, and hurt sales overall. I didn't like the idea of always having to take cash out from a bank machine often located on the street and having to carry large amounts of cash around.

But I guess that is what many people did. My recommendation to travelers would be to find a bank with a cash machine inside like I did and get the cash there for security reasons.

The exchange rate was nine Ukrainian Hrivnas to one U.S. dollar. So often if I withdrew one hundred dollars from the machine I had nine hundred Hrivnas in my wallet in mixed bills. It can be quite a pile of money.

But overall I saw that seventy years of forced atheistic socialism has retarded the economy to such an extent that it will take them years to get up to par with the west. Add this to the distrust of foreigners and many things foreign it makes Ukraine very non competitive on a global scale. Ukraine is among the lowest 10% of competitive countries in Europe just below Macedonia. There is progress, however slow and you do find good customer service in the better restaurants and hotels, but I was at the street level mixing with the locals not rubbing shoulders with the rich.

The businesses that deal primarily with tourists are much better in customer service than other outfits mostly because they have to be. One last note on the economy in the Ukraine, any country that can have mass black outs or power outages and not be able to provide heat to its people for days or even weeks during a very cold bitter winter has to be in deep economic trouble. Ukraine buys natural gas from Russia whose pipeline runs through the Ukraine from the natural gas rich areas of the Caspian Sea and the Caucasus Mountains to mother Russia. The problem is that the country can't always pay what the Russians want. So the Russians threaten and often do cut off the gas. The Ukrainians reply by taking the gas out of the pipes anyway and provide it to its people. This constant struggle are signs of how government run utilities can be inefficient and create shortages temporarily or long term when there really doesn't need to be. Who suffers from this are the simple people, and they suffer from inefficiencies from a socialist economy. A warning to Americans, government run and overregulated utility companies will lead to shortages and blackouts.

# THE WEATHER

I want to mention the weather in the Ukraine because it is important for any traveler to a country. The weather is similar to that in Western Europe but the extremes can be much worse. In the summer it gets hot, from 90-100 Fahrenheit for long periods at a time but what bothered me more was the humidity and the lack of air movement. The air was still and thick in June and July which made it hard to breath. If one is from the East coast then it would be similar but being from California even when it gets that hot the air always moves so you can feel cooler when you sweat. Not in Ukraine, it is just uncomfortable and most places don't have air conditioning so inside is worse than outside. Even many taxi drivers won't turn on the A.C. since it uses too much fuel. To me that is a definition of insanity, when one has A.C. but does not use it and instead chooses to suffer. After a day of sweating the cold shower, due to lack of hot water, was actually refreshing. Now I know how a psychotic in a mental hospital feels. If one must be there in the summer then I recommend heading to the Black Sea since it is a little more comfortable there but it seems like the whole country had the same idea and most beaches are covered with people. We didn't even find a spot on the beach in the Crimean town of Sudak, but it had a wonderful medieval castle built by the Genovese.

As for the winter it comes early, around late October or early November, with the snow falling from about December until March. The first snow like anywhere is beautiful but after the temperatures stay in the negatives for weeks on end winter can be a hard time. It is not as severe and long as the winters in Russia, but remember this is the same winter that stopped the German Wehrmacht in its tracks in the winter of 1941-42, and it is common to have temperatures hit minus 30-40 centigrade. I just don't recommend visiting that time of year because the driving conditions are dangerous since they don't plow the roads like we do in the U.S. Also the sidewalks are always iced over and walking a short distance is dangerous.

I would recommend the fall or spring as the best time to visit. The fall for me is the best time since we don't have a real fall in California like they do back east or in Europe. The leaves change; there is a welcome freshness in the air after a hot summer and it is beautiful in many ways. Even some rain is welcomed after such a summer that we had in 2009. The spring is also nice with all the plants turning green and flowers blooming. I have seen sunflowers before but I have never seen a field of sunflowers so bright yellow and stretching from the road that our bus was on as far as the eye could see. On the opposite side of the same road was a wheat field going the other direction off to the horizon. Now I understand why they called Ukraine the bread basket. These memories are forever etched in my mind. Knowing the history of the Ukraine I realized that these same fields have been the paths of invading armies for centuries and it is hard for one to imagine unless someone has lived it, that such a peaceful place could have been a killing field for thousands. I shuttered at the thought that so many lost their lives here. The list seems endless; the Turks, Vikings, Teutonic Knights, Napoleon's army, and the Germans twice. Today the fields are peaceful but await an uncertain future of a land in the middle of change.

# MEDICINE

No matter what people say about President Obama's universal healthcare and that everyone needs to be taken care of is the wrong way to go about it. Sure everyone should have access to healthcare but to socialize the best healthcare system in the world is just wrong. What makes people want to become doctors or nurses or scientists who discover new cures for diseases? They can say they want to help people and all that but at the end of the day the main motivation is money! It is a too stressful and difficult job not to be rewarded with a good paycheck. Obama said that some people make too much money! Do the people who discover new cures and save lives make too much money? If anything politicians make too much. With the beginning of this new health care bill it takes incentives away from being the best and forces hospitals to go out of business and others to cut back. It takes money away from the healthcare workers and gives it to non elected government bureaucrats. One can argue the complications of providing medical care to a country, but like any other field the best and the brightest are attracted to a field because they can be financially rewarded.

Fast forward seventy years of socialized medicine and what will you see? Well it has already happened in the Ukraine. Doctors and nurses making no more than factory workers per month, understaffed hospitals that don't have the tools or drugs to do the job. One nurse on a floor of twenty five or more patients is not uncommon and doctors who drink on their shift or before their shift is also a common occurrence. If your loved one has to get an operation the doctor gives you a list of what he needs from scalpels to sponges and you must buy them yourself at the pharmacy and bring them to the hospital. Then it would be wise to give the doctor a hundred dollars or so to make sure he does a good job during the operation. If one didn't have the money then maybe they would give a bottle of Vodka to the doctor. Hopefully he would drink it after the operation.

After reading this one might laugh and say this will never happen here. It has already happened in the Ukraine today and starting here in the U.S. After seventy years of socialized medicine with medical workers having no incentive to make profit and do their best and make their hospital better than the rest. All the hospitals are basically the same and you need to know people and be ready to pay extra for a good doctor.

As for ambulances they often times don't get there on time sometimes taking an hour or more to get there! Often times just in time to pronounce someone dead! Not that they don't care but they don't have enough money to pay for enough ambulances, so like everything else there is shortage of emergency response vehicles. On a side note my wife and I watched a grocery store burn and the fire truck didn't get there until it was too late!

All in all I feel that after our experience in Ukraine, when you take a common natural human desire to be the best and successful away all you have left is a mediocre at best mentality. Mediocrity didn't put a man on the moon or invent new cures for diseases.

Of course this bleak of a picture won't happen the day after Obama's healthcare bill takes effect here, but slowly our healthcare which is now the best in the world will deteriorate. It might take years so we won't notice it right away but our children and grandchildren will inherit a broken healthcare system that will be similar to the one that exists in Ukraine and many of the states of the former Soviet Union today.

# POLITICS

The politics in the Ukraine are similar in some ways to the system we have in the U.S. and in other ways quite different. Like many European countries they have many different political parties and to get anything done they have to form coalitions with other parties to get enough votes to pass new laws or elect their candidate to the government.

There are political parties that are religious based, some that are right leaning and still others that are more left. There is even one that wants Ukraine to reunite with Russia. These different political parties on the surface seem to be a good thing to a neutral looking into Ukrainian politics. However many politicians of all parties are corrupt and ignore the law whenever they can. They even try to get the wives of big businessman into their parliament just so the wife can take care of the special interests that got her in. Not to mention she will have a job and a higher social status.

The problem with a fledgling democracy in Ukraine lies in the fact those seventy years of atheistic socialism has made it difficult to understand and accept democracy of the people by the people and for the people. As a matter of fact many people from the older generations, above forty, often lament that they are no longer communist. When something happens in their lives that they don't like they often say," this would never happen in the Soviet Union." I talked to some people before the last election and found out that the reason they voted for the eventual winner Victor Yanykovich was that he was rich therefore he won't steal anymore money from the government. They also said," that the city where he was from, Donetsk, was a lot better off the most of the Ukraine economically." We were in that city for a couple of days and we can verify that. So they think he can make the whole of Ukraine like that. The reasons are many for the better conditions in the Donbass region around the industrial city of Donetsk, but rumors abound about the mafia run area and how much violence and killing happened just after the Soviet Union fell. Of course official reports are scarce. Not too many reporters want to write about such things because they fear for their lives.

So politics in the Ukraine are in some ways different than in the U.S. but it foreshadows a dark future for our politics when opposing schools of thought should be censored if they disagree with the current administration. The writer and radio talk show host Mark Levin calls this soft tyranny. If we too head down the long dark road of socialism then it will be increasingly difficult to come back from. Especially after many generations are brainwashed the ideals or lack of from atheistic communism. We have to resist the ideals of today's government of Obama, Harry Reid and Nancy Pelosi trying to persuade us into believing that big government is the best way for economic prosperity. Ukraine is a prime example that big government policies don't work. They had the biggest government of them all for seventy years, the Soviet Union. It failed and every socialistic government like that has failed because mankind wants freedom and democracy and man is by nature competitive. The only system that allows for that trait to thrive is capitalism. Ukraine has a ways to go when it comes to politics and government but if they keep striving towards capitalism and have unhindered democracy I believe they can be successful. It takes years to throw off the shackles of socialism that become ingrained in a society.

# SPORT IN THE UKRAINE

In the former Soviet Union sport was very important. A lot of money and resources were allocated for sport because they wanted to be successful on the world stage like the Olympics and the World Cup of Soccer. They did this because they wanted to project an image of strength and superiority to the rest of the world that communism and their way of life was superior. The result was a lot of success in the Olympics as well as in soccer.

Since the breakup of the Soviet Union sport in the Ukraine has taken a turn for the worse. Soccer being the number one sport has taken a big hit especially. Officially there wasn't professional soccer in the Soviet Union but teams like the Red Army team were made up of just that, soldiers whose job it was to play soccer. Other teams had players that didn't get paid directly but had all their living expenses taken care of like food, car, and housing, effectively professionals.

Famous Ukrainian team Dynamo Kiev

The olympic flame in Kherson stadium that hasn't burnt in years

The scoreboard at Crystal Kherson which hasn't worked in years

Crystal Kherson in action

When the collapse happened many big teams had problems being able to keep their best players who went west looking for a better life. Since the clubs received money from the government before that, money then dried up and they had to operate like businesses which led to many clubs failing or becoming amateur. Soccer teams like Crystal Kherson in the south eastern city of Kherson have fallen from their heyday in the First Soviet Union Division to the amateur regional division in Ukraine.

The soccer teams in Ukraine are in many ways behind the curve when it comes to running soccer clubs like a business. Many clubs lacked corporate sponsorship and private money coming into the clubs for infrastructure and player development. Some clubs are having such hard times that it is not uncommon to find clubs for sale for absurdly low prices. There was an ad for a club in Kiev, the capital, which was for sale for one hundred dollars. Assuming the new owner would pay off the club's debt and put money into the club. An interesting proposition for a would be soccer club owner.

One can see all around the Ukraine, soccer once was the pride of the country's sports and is now in serious decay. Stadiums that date back to the fifties are dilapidating slowly with little hope for the future. Some have floodlights that don't work and benches that are falling apart. Many still have the cement terraces that haven't been seen in the west in the past twenty years. They are a shadow of their past glory days. The First Ukrainian Division, or Premier League, is a professional league but the sixteen team league has its drawbacks. Many teams don't have good youth development programs or scouting, nor do they have enough money to buy foreign players. So they can't compete with the few big clubs in the country that are fortunate to have money and infrastructure.

UEFA Cup game betweem Metalist Kharkov and Sturm Graz

The ultra modern Donbass Arena in Donetsk

One stark contrast is the city of Donetsk where you have the big club and UEFA Cup champions Shakhtar Donetsk having moved into a brand new fifty thousand seat arena, and across the city Metalurg Donetsk plays in a small stadium that was probably built during the Soviet Union and would be a third or fourth division stadium in the west. However, the Metalurg side did make it to the Qualifikation stage of the Europa League in 2009 only to be knocked out by a traditionally strong club Austria Vienna 5-4 on aggregate. We were at that game in Metalurg Stadium the Ukrainian side had a number of foreign players and played good football. More memorable was the cheap price of the ticket. We had good seats in the midfield for about five dollars for both of us! That is unheard of for a Europa league ticket.

The traditional powerhouses in Ukrainian football are Dynamo Kiev and Shakhtar Donetsk. They both have sponsors and money to spend on player development and infrastructure. The owner of Shakhtar is known in the Ukraine as being possibly the richest man in the Ukraine. Rumors abound on how he got his money.

Dynamo Kiev has a glorious European reputation. They were two times European Cup Winners Cup Champions in 1975, and 1986 as well as UEFA Supercup winners in 1975. They also were Champions league semifinalists in 77', 87', and 99'. The most well known player is Andrey Schevchenko. They play in the historic Valeriy Lobanovsky stadium. The stadium was named after the man who coached them for so many years from the time of the Soviet Union until the modern era. He is well respected by this author. They have a memorial to him just outside the stadium named after him which is a must see for any soccer fan.

Memorial to legendary coach Valeriy Lobanovsky

Metalist loses to Sturm

A few other clubs that are making inroads towards a higher level are Karpaty Lvov, Metalist Kharkov, and Dnepr Dnepropetrovsk. All have or are making appearances in the Europa League formerly the UEFA Cup. This is good for Ukrainian football not just for the money they get for qualifying but for the exposure they get in European competition.

At the Metalist Stadium in Kharkov in August of 2009 I experienced a game between Metalist Kharkov and Sturm Graz from Austria. This was a Europa League qualification game. The stadium was in the middle of renovation for the Euro 2012, which held about forty thousand fans. The crowd was about half that but a good crowd on hand for the game. The atmosphere was electric because the first leg a week earlier in Graz ended 1-1. So there was a good chance Metalist would make an appearance in the group stages. People were talking about," we are heading for Europe." This meant if their team won they would be playing in a four team group with some of Europe's better teams. The team from Kharkov fell short that night losing 1-0 to a better organized and disciplined Sturm Graz side. The people were visibly disappointed and the dream of European competition was over for a year. However, they did make it in 2010.

The new Donbass Arena which is amazing is not only used for Shakhtar's league and European games, but is used for some Ukrainian national team games as well. It will also be used for the Euro 2012 which will be hosted in the Ukraine and Poland. There are already problems with infrastructure and the stadia. They were supposed to have four stadia ready by now in the Ukraine and only two are at this moment. UEFA might limit them to two or three and give the other venue to Poland. Also roads and rail have to be repaired before fans from fourteen countries descend on this East European state. One problem was that the stadium in Lvov that was been built by an Austrian firm stopped construction because the

Ukrainian government didn't pay the Austrian firm what was in the contract so they just stopped and left. The UEFA organizing committee has given these two countries deadlines but they have failed to meet them. Only time will tell if they will be ready for summer 2012.

I personally hope the Ukrainian soccer supporters are good hosts to the foreign football fans. My fear is that every street vendor and barkeep will raise the price of everything to gouge fans for every Euro they can get. Maybe the fans should read this book in preparation for what they will experience?

The hope for Ukrainian soccer in the future is to present themselves as good hosts for the Euro 2012 and reap the economic benefits. This hopefully will improve infrastructure at the clubs in Ukraine at all levels thus helping player development and raising the level of soccer so they will have future success to add onto the success of the past.

Metalurg Donetsk against Austria Vienna

In front of Dynamo Stadium

# WHAT LENIN WANTED

T-34 is a monument to those who fought against
the facists from the city of Donetsk in 1941-1945

What Vladimir Lenin wanted for his new Soviet Socialist Union, that stretched from the Baltic to the Black Sea and all the way to the Pacific, was a classless or one class society that would turn into a utopia. Karl Marx who lived some fifty years earlier espoused the view, "to each according to his means, to each according to his needs". Marx and Lenin both despised capitalism and the rich industrialists that prop it up. In a society during Lenin's time, during the Czar's rule, one could understand the people's discontent, of oppression of free speech and democracy. However Lenin and his cohorts were revolutionaries not statesmen. The problem with revolutionaries is that they know how to start trouble but when and if they get power they don't know how to govern. Once Lenin's revolution overthrew the Czar in 1917 it took about four years for the communists to consolidate power. A little known fact outside the Soviet Union was that the communists had to get rid of all the groups that were against the revolution of 1917. I saw evidence of this in a cemetery in Lvov where there was a whole section of soldiers that fought and died against the Reds. The grave stones dated between 1919-1921. Well after the World War I ended.

"On October 31$^{st}$ and November 1$^{st}$, 1918 (almost 2 weeks before the WW I armistice) Ukrainian units (Sich Riflemen) of the rapidly disintegrating Austrian Army took advantage of the circumstances and occupied the predominately Polish City of Lwow in Galicia, proclaiming it a part of a Socialist Ukrainian Republic. The citizens of Lwow, many of them children, fought off the Ukrainians. Polish army units arrived in a few days to assist the citizens. The fight lasted until November 22$^{nd}$, when the Ukrainians were repelled. Many school children died in this fight and a cemetery in Lwow was created in their honor. The children are known as Orleta (Eaglets). The fighting against Ukrainian forces continued until July, 1919 when the Polish army finally pushed back the Ukrainians (who were weakened by fighting the Bolsheviks on another front) beyond the Zbrucz River" (Mongeon, 2003, para. 7).

"In an attempt to help set up a non-Soviet Ukrainian State, Pilsudski formed an alliance with the Ukrainian Symon Petlura. A combined force of Poles and Ukrainians made it to Kiev in May, 1920, but could not hold the area. General Bulak-Balachowicz was originally from the Wilno area. He was in the Czarist Russian army until the Bolshevik revolution, when he formed units determined to fight the Bolsheviks. He became an ally of Pilsudski and organized units of volunteers made up of Poles from the eastern border areas, which fought in Russia against the Bolsheviks. One of the terms of the 1921 Riga peace treaty between Poland and Russia was the removal of official Polish support for any nationalist groups from Ukraine or Bialy Russia. As a result, Petlura lost Polish support and was defeated by the Bolsheviks. General Bulak-Balachowicz remained in Poland after the War. He died in Warsaw in 1940. He was reputed to have organized an underground unit in Warsaw to fight against the Germans" (Mongeon, 2003, para. 11).

The graves of Ukrainian and Poles who fought against
the Red Army between 1918-1921

Lenin died soon after the formation of the Soviet Union and the reign of terror began. Not to say it would have been much different under Lenin, the man who had the last Czar and his family executed. But under Joseph Stalin, the self named man of steel, millions died who opposed the communist regime. What Lenin wanted was a society where everyone made the same amount of money. Everyone was a comrade and therefore didn't have a higher or lower social class than any other person. They wanted both husband and wife to work in the factories or fields and the state would take care of the children at daycare or schools. All the better for political indoctrination from an early age. There would be no poor or homeless and no rich class ruling over the peasants like it was during the Czar's time. Everything would function because the government would own the means of production. On paper it sounds nice but it is not realistic.

Monument to those who fought the facists in Kherson
during the Great Patriotic War. 1941-1945

On "June 22, 1944. Stalin's Secret document No. 078/42, over the signatures of NKVD chief Beria, Marshal Zhukov and Federov proposes exile to Siberia of "all Ukrainians who had lived under the German occupation". Since all Ukraine was under German occupation this effectively meant every Ukrainian could be exiled except those who had escaped to Russia in 1941. Krushchev in his Secret Speech condemned Stalin for this decree" (Gregorvich, 1995, pg.1)

"KIEV, Ukraine — Veteran Ukrainian nationalist fighters who fought both Soviet and Nazi forces in World War II rallied in the Ukrainian capital Saturday, demanding the same recognition as the Red Army veterans

The nationalists briefly scuffled with opposing socialists, who were holding a counter-rally, but police were largely successful in blocking protesters from clashing. They detained about 20 socialist and nationalist activists who attempted to break through police cordons.

Some 2,000 veteran nationalist fighters and their supporters gathered in front of St. Sophia Cathedral to honor victims of the Ukrainian Insurgent Army, which marked the 64th anniversary of its founding today.

During Soviet times, schoolchildren were taught that members of the Ukrainian Insurgent Army were enemies of the people who committed atrocities alongside Nazi troops. After the 1991 Soviet collapse, the former guerrillas have sought to win financial and moral recognition similar to what Red Army veterans have long enjoyed" (Associated Press, 2006).

Because of history like this there is animosity between Ukrainians themselves. With so many countries bordering the Ukraine, seven in all, they have been caught in so many conflicts. At the time of these events it would have been hard to decide what side to be on without knowing the final outcome.

Some of old Lvov still stands today

# WHAT THE PEOPLE GOT

The promise of Lenin's utopia was not to happen in the Ukraine or for any other part of the Soviet Union. The revolution gave power not to the people, but to a select group who had power for life. Stalin ruled with an iron fist and millions died of starvation in the Ukraine between the years 1932-1933. The great famine was brought about by Stalin's regime to break the will of the Ukrainian people and to kill any desire for independence. This manmade famine was not known in the west until after the fall of the iron curtain and still not many in the west have even heard of it today. There was no shortage of wheat in the Ukraine during those years. The Soviets harvested it and sold it abroad for a very good price. Since at this same time the American farms were in the middle of the great depression and many were negatively affected by the dust bowl. The Soviet government made a profit but the very same people who harvested it were left to starve. Any farmers caught hiding any wheat or produce were arrested and executed. People literally dropped dead walking down the street. This is not my idea of Utopia.

Lenin in Nikoleav

What Ukrainians call "shtuchnyi holod (the man-made famine) or even the Ukrainian holocaust claimed an estimated five to seven million lives. Purely in terms of mortality, it was thus of the same order of magnitude as the Jewish Holocaust. It was, however, a very different kind of genocide in that it was neither motivated by any quest for racial purity, nor was it an attempt to physically murder every single Ukrainian. The purpose, insofar as we may discern it, was to destroy the Ukrainian nation as a political factor and social organism, a goal which could be attained far short of complete extermination" (Bilinsky, 1999)

"Fifty years ago as I write these words, the Ukraine and the Ukrainian, Cossack and other areas to its east—a great stretch of territory with some forty million inhabitants—was like one vast Belsen. A quarter of the rural population, men women and children, lay dead and dying, the rest in various stages of debilitation with no strength to bury their families or neighbors. At the same time (as at Belsen), well-fed squads of police or party officials supervised the victims" (Bilinsky, 1999).

"This was the climax of the "revolution from above," as Stalin put it, in which he and his associates crushed two elements seen as irremediably hostile to the regime: the peasantry of the USSR as a whole, and the Ukrainian nation" (Bilinsky, 1999).

This statue of Lenin for me represents big government
little person. That is what the people got

When a government has great power and the people give control to a central government such as in the Soviet Union they lose most freedoms. Entrepreneurs were not allowed since this is the basis of capitalism and that was the great evil from the west.

What people did get was long work hours for little money and a low standard of living, unless they were part of the government elite. In fact they had a much lower standard of living than other East Bloc countries such as Hungary and Poland. The people got a government run medical system that was years behind the west and even though everyone had access to it, unless you had money or knew someone the wait was long and the care was poor. The doctors and nurses were and still are low paid and over worked. Nurses, for example, make about one hundred dollars a month and doctors not that much more.

Since much money was spent by the Soviet government on military equipment throughout the Cold War, the people saw little creature comforts. It is a simple case of guns or butter economics. Which states, there is only so much money a country has to spend on production so it has to choose between military goods or civilian goods? They chose military goods production. The result was there were very few consumer goods like televisions and toasters. Clothes were also hard to find especially of any variety or fashion. They spent money on infrastructure such as roads, train stations and airports, but they had a secondary military purpose. In times of war all of these things could be used to transport troops and equipment to wherever they needed.

Every city looked basically the same meaning the buildings were built one way. They were built like grey cement blocks. Each city had a Lenin statue and a monument to the Great Patriotic War, which we call World War II. Even the streets were named the same in many cities. They used to tell the people if you travel to another city we want you to feel at home, that is why the cities looked all the same. Nice thought but the reality was that they didn't want people to see one city that was nicer than another since one was allowed to move freely from place to place so that would cause jealousy and discontent which had no place in a socialistic society like the former Soviet Union.

After the fall of the Soviet Union many people lost money they had in the banks because the banks closed and their money was not insured by the government. People now don't trust banks in the Ukraine and it is not uncommon that people hide cash in their apartments and keep it in dollars and not in Hrivna. They have no faith in their own money so they are hungry for dollars. The Hrivna fluctuates too much and one can see a mini panic every time it drops quickly and people will rush to change it into dollars. The banks in response will refuse to exchange dollars for Hrivna or just close. The exchange rate changes daily and the price of goods almost as quickly.

From seventy years of Marxism what the people got was a country that has an aging and decaying infrastructure, a young population that are forced to other countries for work, high unemployment rate, and a week banking and finance system, depleted military, and a medical system that is twenty years behind the west and also broke. All these things this author believes are a direct result of atheistic socialism that has drained Ukraine of resources, hope, desire, and trust of their neighbor let alone their government.

Lenin in Kherson

# HOPE FOR THE FUTURE?

There is hope for the future of Ukraine. There are new buildings being built, stores opening and an economy trying to shake the shackles of their socialist past. They will have to get away from being xenophobic like many people in Ukraine today. This distrust of foreigners comes from the old mentality of the Soviet Union. Where all that was foreign was against the Soviet ideal and foreign influence was looked upon as being a corrupting influence to the people of the Soviet Union. There is a young generation that embraces capitalism and wants democracy but the roadblocks to progress are many.

The government of the Ukraine lead by newly elected Viktor Janykovich needs to do one thing to help the people and the economy. They need to get out of the way and let the private sector do what it does best, create jobs and wealth. This will help get the economy out of its present state.

On November 16, 2010 the government wanted to raise the national sales tax or VAT to more than the current 20%! They also wanted to raise the pensioner's tax, Ukraine's form of social security. The government knows full well that most people don't live longer than sixty five years so many don't even see that money it just gets put into some kind of government fund. In response to this, busloads of private business owners and workers who would be hurt by this increase, were heading to Kiev to protest when the national police force stopped the buses outside the capital and turned them away without any good reason. The government does not want protesters in the streets of the capital. They don't have the right to assemble in a public place, or if so only on paper!

The idea of business is understood by some and lost by others. Some get the idea that one needs to cultivate the business customer relationship. But others still have a Soviet mentality when everyone was owned by the government and one was lucky to find something on the shelves of the stores, and friendly customer assistance was nonexistent. Now there are business people who understand the idea of customer service and others who try to get the most money out of the customer and to hell with them after that!

We had an experience with a hotel that advertised certain amenities and once we checked in and paid up front mind you, because in Ukraine one must pay when you check not when you check out. We found out that these things were in repair or cost extra! The management didn't care if we were unhappy, why should they? After all they had our money!

There is hope for the future if Ukraine gets into the European Union but this won't solve their problems completely, they have to take care of too many things domestically beforehand as I mentioned in this text. The lowering of the tax rate not the raising of it comes to mind. This should also help curtail government corruption. I am a firm believer in that smaller government means less corruption and more opportunity for the people to be free and successful. The ability is there but it will take time and hopefully for the people of Ukraine no more setbacks.

# A LESSON FOR US IN THE U.S.

I see present day Ukraine as the U.S. seventy years from now. What I mean is that Ukraine is the end result of seventy years of atheistic socialism. Like many other former Warsaw Pact countries. Today in the U.S. we see the beginning and rise of socialism, the idea that religion is unimportant or antiquated. This agenda is pushed by the progressive left and has been for the last couple of decades. The disappearance of nativity scenes at schools and government buildings is one example. This is similar to how religion was suppressed and put down in the Soviet Union, for example they turned churches into gyms to play basketball in during the time of the U.S.S.R. In America it is not so obvious yet.

As for the economy we see a rise in socialistic ideas and policies, like Obamacare and cap in trade. Many of our own elected officials seemed to not have paid attention in school when it came to History and Economics or they choose to ignore the facts. Communistic socialism failed in a big way yet many politicians in our country today think that they can take from the public trough and that it is bottomless. The fact that the two biggest socialist regimes, U.S.S.R and Nazi Germany, had to kill millions of people who didn't go alone with their system is clear proof that a powerful centralized government is contradictory to freedom and democracy. We should also learn that raising taxes is almost always a bad idea for the economy because it takes money from the system that could be invested, saved or spent by the public which in every aspect helps create new wealth. The government never creates new wealth it only reallocates it.

If America continues on this path of big government, increasing the number of government programs and control, they will destroy the greatest economic engine the world has ever seen. The destruction of an economy doesn't happen overnight but overtime. In Ukraine government medicine, factories, and transportation are all inefficient and provide poor service to the people. We should look at these examples of a failed system and strive not to follow them done this path.

The people of the U.S. have to understand that government doesn't know how to use your money better than you. That most things government run is inefficient and lacks the quality that the same thing would have if produced and provided by the private sector.

This author contends that politicians who propose socialistic programs and ideals just want more power and money. With increased size of government comes more money for more government jobs and therefore have more power over people's everyday lives. They also are less tolerant to contrasting political views because they view them as a threat, not as other ideas. They understand that socialism can only exist in a vacuum and not with other competing systems. It cannot exist in a world that has capitalism because it cannot compete. Socialism must destroy capitalism to exist, but capitalism does not need to destroy socialism to exist. That is why people that truly believe in socialism and take it to the extreme are a danger to a free and democratic country.

# REFERENCES

Associated Press. (2006). *Ukrainian World War II Anti-Soviet Fighters Demand Recognition as Vets.* Retrieved August 1, 2011, from: http://www.foxnews.com/story/0,2933,220819,00.html

Bilinsky, Y. (1999). *Journal of Genocide Recearch.* Retrieved August 1, 2011, from: http://www.faminegenocide.com/resources/bilinsky.html

Gregorvich, A. (1995). *World war II in Ukraine:Chronology of the War in Ukraine.* Retrieved August 1, 2011, from: http://www.infoukes.com/history/ww2/page-28.html

Hannity, S. (2010). *Conservative Victory.* Harper Collins Publishers. New York.

Levin, M. R. (2009). *Liberty and Tyranny.* Threshold Editions. A Division of Simon and Schuster, Inc. New York.

Mongeon, A. (2003). *The Polish-Russian War and the fight for independence, 1918-1921.* Retrieved August 1, 2011, from: http://home.golden.net/~medals/1918-1921war.html

www.kicker.de—German Football magazine website. 2011

www.ingramcontent.com/pod-product-compliance
Lightning Source LLC
Chambersburg PA
CBHW061222280526
45784CB00006B/2597

* 9 7 8 1 4 6 5 3 4 9 7 3 6 *